As the Mill Wheel Turns

Tasty, Traditional Biscuits & Breads

Patricia B. Mitchell

Portions of this manuscript were originally published under the title *Crumbs Between the Covers*, copyright © 1994 by Patricia B. Mitchell.

Published 1999 by the author.
Mail: Mitchells, Box 429, Chatham, VA 24531
Book Sales: 800-967-2867
E-mail: *Answers@FoodHistory.com*
Websites: *FoodHistory.com* and *MitchellsPublications.com*

Compact Edition
Printed in the U.S.A.
ISBN-10: 0-925117-97-8
ISBN-13: 978-0-925117-97-7

Seventh Printing, September 2013

- *Illustrations* -

Front Cover Vignette – detail from "Old Mill on Beaver Creek," Krebs Lithographing Company, Cincinnati, Ohio, 1879, provided by the Library of Congress. Woodgrain frame is provided by Dover Publications, Inc., New York. Background is from a weathered plank.

Inside Title Page – "The Woman Who Will Read," an illustration from Mrs. Julia McNair Wright, *The Ideal Home*, 1897, facing p. 333.

Page 36 – detail adapted from "The Old Grist Mill," etching published by Edwin Forbes in a portfolio entitled *Life Studies of the Great Army*, 1876, provided by Dover Publications, Inc.

Back Cover – "The Old Mill Stream" by Gibson, provided by the Library of Congress.

Cover design and illustration research are by Sarah E. Mitchell, *VintageDesigns.com*.

Table of Contents

Introduction

"Bad bread wrecks my outlook on life," wrote Jeffrey Steingarten in *The Man Who Ate Everything*.[1] He also remarked: "Bread [good bread] is the only food I know that satisfies completely, all by itself. It comforts the body, charms the senses, gratifies the soul and excites the mind."[2] I concur! And behind the bread is the baker, and behind the baker is the miller and the mill.

Nowadays most commercial flour is processed in huge factory-like facilities. Complex, sleek electricity-powered machinery mills and packages standardized flour mixtures. Human hands and personalities seem far removed from this industrialized operation. Nevertheless, there are, thank goodness, a few old-fashioned millers and mills still in operation. At these historic mills the miller is personally involved in every aspect of the milling process, making countless decisions daily about the grinding of grains and the "turning of the mill wheel."

This cookbook contains some of our family's favorite bread recipes. Although "grocery store" flours work fine, use stone-ground flour and meal whenever you can for more flavor and nutrition. Remember, however, that your locally milled, old-timey flour or cornmeal might "behave" differently than a standardized national brand. Because the moisture content of flours can vary considerably, it may be necessary to adjust the amount of liquid in a particular recipe.

Ovens and bread pans/baking sheets create "variables," too. For example, I often have to "flip over" biscuits mid-baking time because the bottoms are getting too dark. Is it the oven, the baking sheet? I dunno.

Whole Wheat Biscuits

1 c. whole wheat flour
1 c. all-purpose flour

1 tbsp. baking powder
$^3/_4$ tsp. salt
$^1/_4$ c. solid shortening
$^2/_3$ to $^3/_4$ c. milk

Combine dry ingredients with shortening until like coarse crumbs. In bowl make a well; add milk all at once. Stir quickly with fork, only until dough follows fork around bowl. Turn dough onto lightly floured surface. Knead gently 10 to 11 strokes ($^1/_2$ minute). Roll or pat dough $^1/_2$ inch thick. Dip biscuit cutter in flour, cut straight down — no twisting. Bake on ungreased baking sheet for 12 to 15 minutes at 450° F. Yield: 16 biscuits.[3]

Drop of Sunshine Biscuits

2 c. cornmeal (Use plain — not self-rising — cornmeal in my
   recipes, unless otherwise noted.)
2 c. whole wheat flour
2 tsp. baking powder
$^1/_2$ tsp. salt
3 tbsp. sugar
2 tbsp. orange peel, finely chopped
$^1/_4$ c. mild-flavored olive *or* vegetable oil
2 c. (approximately) milk (Reconstituted non-fat milk is fine.)

Combine the dry ingredients. In a separate container, mix the oil and milk. Stir together the two mixtures well. Drop large spoonfuls of the dough on baking sheets. Bake at 400° F. for about 12 minutes, then, if they are getting "toasty" on the bottom, turn them over and bake a little longer until golden brown.

Our family of five normally eats three meals (and bedtime snacks) at home every day of the week. (We have home businesses and do home schooling.) We also feed Bed & Breakfast guests and friends. At almost every meal and snack we have home-baked bread stuffs of some sort, so you see I had better like to bake! (We do eat out, occasionally!)

Three Grain Biscuits

$1\frac{1}{2}$ c. whole wheat flour
1 c. unbleached *or* all-purpose flour
1 c. cornmeal
1 c. quick oats
4 tsp. baking powder
$\frac{1}{2}$ tsp. salt
3 tbsp. olive *or* vegetable oil
$1\frac{1}{2}$ c. (approx.) milk

Proceed as in the preceding recipe.

Alternative Oat Drop Biscuits

$2\frac{1}{2}$ c. quick *or* old-fashioned oats
$1\frac{1}{2}$ c. whole wheat flour
1 tbsp. baking powder
$\frac{1}{2}$ tsp. salt
$1\frac{2}{3}$ to 2 c. milk
1 tbsp. olive *or* vegetable oil
1 tbsp. molasses
$\frac{1}{2}$ to $\frac{3}{4}$ c. raisins (optional)

Mix the first four ingredients. Then mix the remaining items, using the lesser amount of milk, unless more is needed. Combine the two mixtures, and bake at 400° F. for 12 to 15 minutes, turning them over once.

Patriotic Rye Drop Biscuits

The recipe upon which this recipe is based was developed during World War I. The idea was to use part rye flour, thus conserving more wheat flour for the boys in uniform.

2 c. rye flour
1 c. whole wheat flour
1 c. unbleached *or* all-purpose flour
1 tbsp. baking powder
1 tbsp. sugar
$^{1}/_{2}$ tsp. salt
3 tbsp. olive *or* vegetable oil
Milk

Combine the dry ingredients. In a separate bowl mix a cup of milk and the oil. Stir the dry ingredients into this, adding more milk as needed. Drop big spoonfuls of the dough onto a baking sheet, and bake at 425° F. for about 10 minutes. Turn the heat down to 400° F., turn the biscuits over, and bake 5 to 10 more minutes or until done.

Shredded Wheat Biscuits

2 c. crushed shredded wheat cereal
2 c. milk
3 tbsp. olive *or* vegetable oil
1$^{1}/_{2}$ c. whole wheat flour
2 tsp. baking powder
$^{1}/_{4}$ tsp. salt
2 to 4 tbsp. sweetener (sugar, honey, molasses, syrup, your choice)

Combine the shreds of wheat, the milk, and oil. (If the sweetener chosen is wet, add it to the liquids now. If the sweetener is dry, add it to the dry ingredients being combined in the step below.) Let sit. Meanwhile, combine the dry ingredients. Stir together the two mixtures, adding more milk if necessary to make a soft mixture. Spoon by large spoonfuls onto baking sheets. Bake at 400° F. for about 12 minutes, then turn them over and bake 5 more minutes.

Peppery Parmesan Biscuits

3 c. whole wheat flour
1 tbsp. baking powder
$\frac{1}{2}$ tsp. baking soda
$\frac{1}{4}$ tsp. salt
1 tsp. black pepper (or less to suit taste)
$\frac{1}{2}$ c. Parmesan cheese, grated
2 tbsp. olive or vegetable oil
1$\frac{1}{2}$ c. buttermilk or sour milk (or more)

Combine dry things. Mix milk and oil. Stir together the two mixtures well. Drop by tablespoons onto lightly greased baking sheets. Bake at 425° F. for about 12 minutes, then turn them over and bake until lightly browned.

Note: To create a pint of sour milk, put 2 tbsp. vinegar or lemon juice into a pint measuring cup. Add milk to make 2 cups. Let sit a few minutes until the milk has clabbered.

Mistress Biscuit Mix

I used to call this Master Biscuit Mix, but I reduced the salt in the recipe, and changed the name to Mistress Biscuit Mix.

* * *

4 c. unbleached or all-purpose flour
4 c. whole wheat flour
$\frac{1}{3}$ c. baking powder
2 tsp. salt

Combine the above ingredients. Store in refrigerator or freezer.

Puffed-Up Italian Biscuits

These airy and tempting biscuits are close kin to Peppery Parmesan Biscuits (p. 5), with the added flavor and crunch of sesame seeds. — This recipe makes a big batch. (But then, you've noticed that I tend to think big when it comes to breads!)

* * *

4 c. Mistress Biscuit Mix (on p. 5)
$1/2$ c. Parmesan cheese, grated
2 tbsp. sesame seeds
$1/4$ c. olive *or* vegetable oil
$1 1/2$ c. milk (more or less)

Mix the dry ingredients. Combine the oil and milk and pour into the dry things. Stir to moisten, adding additional milk if need be. Drop by generous spoonfuls onto baking sheets, and bake at 425° F. for 8 to 10 minutes or until the bottoms brown lightly, then turn 'em over and bake a few more minutes for good measure.

Sage and Cheddar Tawny Biscuits

Cheddar cheese jazzes up these flavorful edibles.

* * *

4 c. whole wheat flour
1 tbsp. baking powder
$1/2$ tsp. salt
4 tsp. dry powdered sage

1 c. extra sharp Cheddar cheese, grated
$1/4$ c. olive *or* vegetable oil
2 c. milk

To make these drop biscuits, mix the first four ingredients. In a separate bowl stir together the cheese, oil, and milk. Combine the mixtures well, and drop generous spoonfuls of the batter onto baking sheets. Bake at 425° F. for around 12 minutes or until the bottoms begin to brown, then flip them, and bake about 5 more minutes, depending upon size.

Angel Yeast Biscuits

In the 1800's, yeast was often used to make biscuits. Around the time of the Civil War, baking powder began to be used. The following recipe is a popular composite of the old and the new.

* * *

5 c. unbleached *or* all-purpose flour (can use half whole wheat flour)
2 tsp. baking powder
1 tsp. salt
1 tsp. baking soda
$\frac{1}{4}$ c. sugar
1 c. shortening
1 pkg. baking yeast
2 tbsp. warm water
2 c. buttermilk *or* sour milk
2 to 3 tbsp. melted butter *or* margarine

Mix the dry ingredients; cut in shortening. Dissolve the yeast in the 2 tbsp. warm water. After 5 minutes, stir the yeast mixture into the buttermilk. Add the liquid mixture to the dry mixture and stir well. (At this point you may refrigerate the dough overnight or roll it out immediately. If you refrigerate it, let it sit at room temperature for 2 hours before proceeding.) Turn the dough out on a floured board and roll or pat to desired thickness. Cut out biscuits and place on greased sheets. Brush with melted butter. Bake at 400° F. until golden brown.

Whole Wheat Muffins

$1\frac{1}{2}$ c. whole wheat flour
$\frac{1}{2}$ c. unbleached *or* all-purpose flour

1 tbsp. baking powder
$\frac{1}{2}$ tsp. salt
$\frac{1}{4}$ c. sugar
1 egg, beaten
1 c. milk
2 tbsp. melted butter

    Mix dry ingredients; add egg, milk, and butter. Beat well. Bake in greased muffin tins for 25 to 30 minutes at 400° F.[4]

Blueberry Muffins

2 c. whole wheat, unbleached, *or* all-purpose flour (or a combination)
$\frac{1}{4}$ tsp. salt
2 tsp. baking powder
$\frac{1}{4}$ c. butter
$\frac{1}{2}$ c. sugar
2 eggs, separated
1 c. milk
1 c. blueberries

    Combine the flour, salt, and baking powder. Cream the butter and add the sugar; add the well-beaten egg yolks. Add the dry ingredients alternately with the milk. Roll the berries in flour and stir them into the batter. Add the egg whites, beaten to a stiff froth. Bake in greased muffin pans at 350° F. for 15 minutes.

Rhubarb Muffins

$1\frac{1}{4}$ c. brown sugar, packed
$\frac{1}{2}$ c. olive *or* vegetable oil
1 egg
2 tsp. vanilla
1 c. buttermilk
$1\frac{1}{2}$ c. rhubarb, diced or minced
$\frac{1}{2}$ c. chopped nuts
$2\frac{1}{2}$ c. flour (use partly whole wheat)

1 tsp. baking soda
1 tsp. baking powder
$^1/_2$ tsp. salt

In a large bowl combine the first five ingredients and beat well. With spoon stir in rhubarb and nuts. In separate bowl combine all dry ingredients. Stir into rhubarb mixture just until blended. Spoon batter into 20 greased, medium-sized muffin cups, filling each cup two-thirds full.

Topping:

$^1/_3$ c. sugar
1 tsp. cinnamon
1 tbsp. melted butter

Combine sugar, cinnamon and butter. Sprinkle over filled muffin cups and press lightly into batter. Bake at 400° F. for 20 to 25 minutes.[5]

Raisin - Nut Loaf (or Muffins)

$2^1/_2$ c. Mistress Biscuit Mix (see p. 5)
$^1/_4$ c. sugar
$^3/_4$ c. pecans *or* walnuts, chopped
$^1/_2$ c. raisins
2 tbsp. olive *or* vegetable oil
1 tbsp. orange peel, finely chopped
$1^1/_4$ c. milk

Mix dry ingredients. Combine oil and milk, and stir into the dry ingredients. Spoon into a greased loaf pan or muffin tins. Bake loaf at 350° F. for about 40 minutes or until it tests done. Bake muffins at 400° F. for about 15 minutes.

A Sense of Power

My kitchen does not contain a dishwasher, microwave, food processor, or bread machine. I have almost never even used any of those modern appliances, except for loading dishes into a dishwasher (after I had followed the directive to first wash them!).

I do use a stove and a refrigerator, so see, I have at least one foot in the 20th century! (My goodness, it's already over and I just got here!) The somewhat old-fashioned ways appeal to me, though. I like to chop food by hand. I knead bread because I love the feel, the smell, the color of bread dough. Working with it is a sensual, constructive pleasure. Stirring a batter for a quick bread or biscuits is relaxing, and plopping out dollops of dough on a baking sheet for drop biscuits is fun!

Peeping into the oven to monitor a bread's progress gives me a "responsible rabbit" feeling and a sense of power. A good batch of bread demonstrates a baker's understanding of, and dominion over, the ingredients. Baking well is a victory.

Rice Loaf (or Muffins)

A clever and delicious way to utilize leftover rice!

* * *

2 c. flour (I use whole wheat.)
1 tbsp. baking powder
$\frac{1}{2}$ tsp. salt
3 tbsp. sugar
1 c. cooked rice, at room temperature (I use brown rice.)
1 egg, beaten
$1\frac{1}{3}$ c. milk
3 tbsp. olive *or* vegetable oil

Mix dry things. In another bowl stir together the rice, egg, milk, and oil. Combine the mixtures and spoon into a prepared 9x5-inch bread pan or greased muffin tins. For loaf bread bake at 350° F. for approximately 40 minutes. For muffins bake at 400° F. for about 20 minutes or until done.

International Bread Lore

Traditional scones are triangular-shaped small breads, created by cutting a round loaf into wedges ("farls" or fourth part, or quarters) before baking. They are like biscuits minus the fat. Originally they were baked on griddles and could be made of oats, barley, whole wheat or white flour. They were probably first made in Scotland, and they bear a resemblance to Irish soda bread.

Nowadays, scones are usually baked in the oven. Many people add sugar, dried fruits, and butter or shortening. The enhancements (especially the fat) change the sturdy texture and taste of this olden bread.[6]

Shredded Wheat and Cheese Scones

3 c. whole wheat flour
2 tsp. baking powder
1 tsp. baking soda
$\frac{1}{2}$ tsp. salt
$\frac{1}{2}$ tsp. caraway seeds
3 tbsp. olive *or* vegetable oil
$1\frac{1}{2}$ c. buttermilk *or* sour milk
1 c. shredded wheat cereal, crumbled
1 c. yellow cheese, grated

Combine the first five ingredients. In a separate bowl mix the oil and milk. Combine the two mixtures, and then stir in the crumbled cereal and cheese. Knead slightly, and form two balls. On a flat surface flatten the balls to disks about $\frac{3}{4}$ inch thick. Cut each disk into 8 or more wedge-shaped pieces. Place on baking sheets, and bake at 375° F. for about 10 minutes; then turn the scones over and bake 5 minutes more. Yield: 16 or more scones.

Potato - Cornmeal Triangles

These goodies are similar to an Irish potato bread called fadge. (The Irish leave out the cornmeal and oil.)

* * *

2 c. thoroughly mashed potatoes
$^1/_2$ to $^3/_4$ c. milk (approx.)
3 tbsp. olive *or* vegetable oil
2 c. cornmeal
1 c. unbleached *or* all-purpose flour
4 tsp. baking powder
$^1/_2$ tsp. salt

Mix the first three ingredients, reserving part of the milk. Mix the dry ingredients, and stir into the mashed mixture, adding more milk if necessary to make a workable dough. Form two or three disks, and cut into wedges. Bake at 400° F. for 10 minutes, then turn them over and bake about 10 more minutes.

Following are recipes for some delicious, do-ahead-of-time loaf breads.

Pigeon Forge Brown Bread

2 c. whole wheat flour
1 c. cornmeal
1 tsp. baking soda
$^1/_2$ tsp. salt
$^3/_4$ c. raisins
$^1/_2$ c. molasses
$1^3/_4$ to 2 c. buttermilk *or* sour milk

Mix dry things. Add molasses and milk and stir together well. Pour into a 9x5-inch bread pan, the inside bottom of which has been greased. Bake at 350° F. for about 40 minutes.

Note: Pigeon Forge, a hospitable town in east Tennessee, is home to the fun "Dollywood" theme park.

Quick Brown Raisin Bread

1½ c. whole wheat flour
1 c. unbleached *or* all-purpose flour
1 tsp. baking soda
½ tsp. baking powder
¼ tsp. salt
½ tsp. cinnamon
½ tsp. ginger
2 tbsp. sugar
2 tsp. orange peel, finely chopped
½ c. raisins
2 tbsp. olive *or* vegetable oil
2 tbsp. molasses
1 egg, beaten
1 to 1¼ c. buttermilk *or* sour milk

Mix dry ingredients, then mix remaining items. Combine the mixtures. Spoon into a 9x5-inch loaf pan, the inside bottom of which has been greased. Bake at 350° F. for approximately 35 minutes or until a toothpick inserted near the center of the loaf comes out unsticky. (Ovens and flours vary, so baking times are only estimates.)

Bread Break Raisin Bran Bread

This bread is nice for a snack when topped with honey.

* * *

3¼ c. whole wheat flour
2½ c. wheat bran
1 tsp. baking soda
1 c. raisins
½ c. molasses
3¼ c. milk
1½ tbsp. vinegar (add last)

Combine dry ingredients. In a separate bowl combine molasses and milk. Mix together the two mixtures, add vinegar, and spoon into two bread pans, the inside bottoms of which have been greased. Bake at 350° F. for approximately 40 minutes.

Multi-Grain Bread

1 c. cornmeal
1 c. rye flour
1 c. whole wheat flour
1 tsp. baking powder
$1/2$ tsp. baking soda
2 tbsp. sugar
$1/4$ tsp. salt
$1/2$ c. raisins (optional)
3 tbsp. molasses
$1^1/_2$ to $1^2/_3$ c. sour milk

Follow the same procedure as for Quick Brown Raisin Bread on the preceding page, baking longer if necessary.

Southern Innkeeper's Oat Bran - Prune Loaves

$2^1/_2$ c. quick oats
2 c. oat bran
$2^1/_2$ c. whole wheat flour
2 tsp. baking powder
$1/2$ tsp. salt
$2/_3$ c. sugar
1 tsp. cinnamon
$1^1/_2$ c. cooked pitted prunes, cut up
2 tbsp. olive *or* vegetable oil
4 c. milk

Combine dry ingredients. In a separate bowl combine the liquids. Mix together the two mixtures, and spoon into two 9x5-inch pans, the inside bottoms of which have been greased. Bake at 350° F. for approximately 40 minutes.

Prune - Apple Loaf

2 1/2 c. whole wheat flour
2 tsp. baking powder
1/2 tsp. baking soda
1/4 tsp. salt
1 tsp. cinnamon
1/2 tsp. allspice
1/4 tsp. cloves
1/3 c. brown sugar, packed
1 1/2 c. cooked pitted prunes, cut up
2 tbsp. olive *or* vegetable oil
1 1/3 c. buttermilk *or* sour milk
2/3 c. raw apple, chopped

Combine the dry ingredients. In a separate bowl, mix the remaining ingredients. Stir together the two mixtures. Spoon the batter into a 9x5-inch loaf pan, the inside bottom of which has been greased, and bake at 350° F. for around 50 minutes.

Almond and Prune Loaf

1 c. uncooked pitted prunes, cut up
2 1/4 c. boiling water
3 tbsp. olive *or* vegetable oil
2 1/4 c. whole wheat flour
1 c. unbleached *or* all-purpose flour
2 tsp. baking powder
1/2 tsp. salt
1/3 c. sugar
1/4 c. dry milk powder (unreconstituted)
1/2 c. slivered almonds

Combine the cut-up prunes, boiling water, and oil and let sit for 30 minutes. Meanwhile, mix the dry ingredients. Combine the two groups, and spoon into a 9x5-inch bread pan, the inside bottom of which has been greased. Bake at 350° F. for 40 to 45 minutes, or until a toothpick inserted near the center comes out unsticky.

The Regal Master

One of my favorite stories about a bread maker involves Lucretia Garfield, President James A. Garfield's wife. Long before she became First Lady, Lucretia had to cook and care for a household of five children and a husband. She decided to overcome her dislike for the chore of bread-making by taking a special interest in it. She wrote:

"The whole of life became brighter. The very sunshine seemed to be flowing down through my spirit into the white loaves, and now I believe my table is furnished with better bread than ever before; and this truth, as old as creation, seems just now to have become fully mine — that I need not be the shrinking slave of toil, but its regal master." [7]

Quick Allspice Orange - Nut Bread

$2^1/_2$ c. whole wheat flour
$^1/_2$ c. unbleached *or* all-purpose flour
1 tsp. baking powder
$^1/_2$ tsp. baking soda
$^1/_4$ tsp. salt
$^1/_2$ tsp. allspice
$^1/_3$ c. sugar
2 tbsp. orange peel, finely chopped
1 c. nuts, chopped (pecans, walnuts, or your pleasure)
2 tbsp. olive *or* vegetable oil
$1^1/_3$ c. orange juice
$^3/_4$ c. water

Mix the dry ingredients. In a separate bowl stir together the liquids. Combine the two mixtures, and spoon into a 9x5-inch pan, the inside bottom of which has been greased. If possible, let the loaf sit 20 or 30 minutes before baking — an especially good practice with breads containing nuts. (Supposedly the "rest period" decreases the risk of the characteristic "crack" along the top of nut bread loaves.) Bake at 350° F. for about 40 minutes, or until bread tests done.

Orange Raisin Loaf

1 c. unbleached *or* all-purpose flour
1 c. whole wheat flour
$\frac{3}{4}$ c. wheat germ
$\frac{1}{4}$ c. sugar
2 tsp. baking powder
$\frac{1}{2}$ tsp. salt
$\frac{3}{4}$ c. raisins
$1\frac{1}{3}$ c. milk
3 tbsp. olive *or* vegetable oil
1 tbsp. orange peel, finely chopped

Mix dry ingredients. In a different container mix remaining things. Stir together the two mixtures. Spoon into a 9x5-inch loaf pan, the inside bottom of which has been greased. Bake at 350° F. for about 40 minutes.

Orange Bran Bread

$1\frac{1}{4}$ c. wheat bran
$1\frac{1}{2}$ c. orange juice
$\frac{1}{4}$ c. olive *or* vegetable oil
1 egg, beaten
1 tbsp. orange peel, finely chopped
1 tsp. vanilla
2 c. whole wheat flour
$\frac{1}{2}$ c. quick oats
3 tbsp. sugar
$\frac{1}{4}$ c. wheat germ
1 tbsp. baking powder
$\frac{1}{4}$ tsp. cinnamon

Combine bran, orange juice, oil, egg, orange peel, and vanilla. Meanwhile, mix the remaining dry ingredients. Combine the two mixtures, stirring just until moist. Spoon into a loaf pan, the inside bottom of which has been greased. Bake at 350° F. for 45 to 50 minutes.

Pennsylvania Dutch Applesauce Bread

This is one of the first quick loaf breads I learned to make — a "newlywed recipe" we still cherish. Nowadays, I suggest using mild olive oil, rather than shortening.

* * *

$^1\!/_4$ c. shortening, *or* mild olive *or* vegetable oil
$^1\!/_2$ to $^2\!/_3$ c. sugar
2 eggs
1 tsp. vanilla

Either use 2 c. self-rising flour or:

2 c. unbleached *or* all-purpose flour (you can use half whole wheat flour)
1 tsp. baking powder
1 tsp. salt
1 tsp. baking soda

2 tsp. cinnamon
1 c. applesauce
$^1\!/_2$ c. walnuts, chopped (optional)

Cream shortening and sugar. Beat in eggs and vanilla. Blend in dry ingredients. Add applesauce (and nuts). Pour into a 9x5-inch loaf pan, the inside bottom of which has been greased. Let rest 20 minutes. Bake at 350° F. for 55 minutes.

Maple Graham Bread

This is a satisfying, gratifying bread you'll want again and again!

* * *

$2^1\!/_2$ c. buttermilk *or* sour milk
$^1\!/_2$ tsp. baking soda

²/₃ c. maple syrup
¹/₂ tsp. salt
3¹/₂ c. whole wheat flour
1 c. raisins
2 tsp. baking powder

Combine milk, baking soda, and maple syrup. Stir in salt, flour, and raisins. Add baking powder. Mix well. Spoon into a 9x5-inch loaf pan, the inside bottom of which has been greased. Bake at 350° F. for 45 to 50 minutes.

Fort Worth Oat Loaf

This bread has a dense texture — it's reminiscent of a European peasant loaf. I love it. My kids and I joke, though, that you need a chain saw to slice it.

* * *

1¹/₂ c. unbleached *or* all-purpose flour
1¹/₂ c. whole wheat flour
2 c. quick oats
3 tbsp. brown sugar, packed
1 tbsp. baking powder
1 tsp. baking soda
¹/₄ tsp. salt
³/₄ tsp. cinnamon
1¹/₄ c. buttermilk *or* sour milk
2 tbsp. olive *or* vegetable oil

Mix the dry things. Make a well in the center and stir in the milk and oil, adding a little more milk if the mixture is impossibly dry. (It should be barely moist.) Spoon this rather stiff dough into a 9x5-inch bread pan, the inside bottom of which has been greased. Bake at 350° F. for around 35 minutes, or until lightly browned.

Graham Bread

Another "chain-saw" bread which I really like is Graham Bread. (My maiden name is Beaver, so it's no wonder I enjoy chewy, crunchy, or interestingly-textured foods!)

* * *

2 c. graham (whole wheat) flour
2 c. unbleached *or* all-purpose flour
4 tsp. baking powder
$1/2$ tsp. salt
3 tbsp. sugar
$1^2/_3$ c. milk (more or less may be necessary)

Mix the dry ingredients, and add enough milk to make dough the consistency of biscuit dough. Form into a loaf and place in a 9x5-inch loaf pan, the inside bottom of which has been lightly greased. Bake at 350° F. for around 40 minutes or until firm.

Harvest Bread

The cheese in this recipe is the "secret" ingredient. It adds a mellow undertone.

* * *

$2^3/_4$ c. whole wheat flour
1 tsp. baking soda
$1/2$ tsp. salt
$1/4$ c. sugar
2 c. buttermilk *or* sour milk
$1/4$ c. olive *or* vegetable oil
1 egg, beaten
$1^1/_2$ c. raw apples, cored and finely chopped
$3/4$ c. Cheddar cheese, grated
$1/2$ c. walnuts, chopped

Combine the first four ingredients. In a separate bowl, beat together the milk, oil, and egg. Stir together the two mixtures. Fold in the apples, cheese, and walnuts. Spoon into a 9x5-inch loaf pan, the inside bottom of which has been greased. (If possible, let the batter sit in the loaf pan 20 to 30 minutes before baking.) Bake at 350° F. for about 50 minutes.

Hidden Hazelnut Bread

This dreamy Hidden Hazelnut Bread blankets your taste buds with the flavor of spices, apple, and hazelnuts.

* * *

$2^1/_2$ c. whole wheat flour
$^1/_2$ c. wheat bran (optional)
$^1/_3$ c. sugar
2 tsp. baking powder
$^1/_4$ tsp. salt
1 tsp. baking soda
1 tsp. cinnamon
$^1/_2$ tsp. allspice
$^1/_4$ tsp. cloves
2 c. milk
2 tbsp. olive *or* vegetable oil
$^3/_4$ c. raw apples, chopped
$^1/_2$ c. raisins
$^1/_4$ c. hazelnuts (also called filberts), chopped

Mix the dry ingredients. In another bowl mix the milk, oil, apple, and raisins. Stir the dry ingredients into the wet mixture. Fold in the hazelnuts. Spoon the batter into a 9x5-inch loaf pan, the inside bottom of which has been greased. Bake at 350° F. for around 45 minutes.

Walnut Raisin Bread

$2^1/_4$ c. whole wheat flour
2 tsp. baking soda

1 tsp. baking powder
1/4 tsp. salt
1/2 c. sugar
1 c. quick oats
3/4 c. raisins
1/3 c. walnuts, chopped
2 c. buttermilk *or* sour milk

Mix the dry ingredients. In a separate bowl, mix the wet ingredients. Combine. Spoon into a 9x5-inch loaf pan, the inside bottom of which has been greased. Bake at 350° F. for approximately 40 minutes.

Zucchini Zinger Bread

The following is one of our children's favorite bed-time snacks.

* * *

2 c. zucchini squash, peeled and grated
1/2 c. olive *or* vegetable oil
1/2 c. brown sugar, packed
2 eggs, beaten
2 tsp. vanilla
1 c. raisins
3 c. whole wheat flour
1 tsp. baking powder
1 tsp. baking soda
1/2 tsp. salt
1 tsp. nutmeg
1 tbsp. cinnamon

Mix together the first six ingredients. In a different bowl, mix the remaining six ingredients. Combine the mixtures, and stir until moistened. Turn batter into two 9x5-inch bread pans, the inside bottoms of which have been greased. Bake at 350° F. for about 45 minutes or until a toothpick inserted near the center of the loaves comes out clean.

Rhineland Sweet Bread

This is my recipe for a sweet bread (not as dessert-like as some, but mighty good, if I do say so myself!). Perfect warm at breakfast or cool at snack-attack time.

* * *

2 c. whole wheat flour
1 c. quick oats
2 tsp. baking powder
$\frac{1}{4}$ tsp. salt
$\frac{1}{4}$ tsp. baking soda
$1\frac{1}{3}$ c. apple butter
2 tbsp. olive *or* vegetable oil
1 egg, beaten
$1\frac{1}{3}$ c. milk
$\frac{2}{3}$ c. raisins

Combine dry ingredients. In a separate container mix the wet things, including the raisins. Stir together the two batches. Pour batter into a 9x5-inch loaf pan, the inside bottom of which has been greased. Mix together topping (recipe follows) and sprinkle the topping onto the batter. Pat in gently, and then bake at 350° F. for 55 to 60 minutes.

Topping:

$\frac{1}{4}$ c. quick oats
1 tbsp. sugar
1 tbsp. butter *or* margarine, melted

Mix together.

Toasty Coconut Bread

2 c. whole wheat flour
1 c. unbleached *or* all-purpose flour

1 tbsp. baking powder
$\frac{1}{2}$ tsp. salt
2 tbsp. sugar
$\frac{1}{4}$ c. flaked coconut
$\frac{1}{4}$ c. slivered almonds
2 tsp. lemon peel, grated
1 egg, beaten
1 c. applesauce
$\frac{1}{4}$ tsp. almond extract (optional)
2 tbsp. olive *or* vegetable oil
$1\frac{1}{2}$ c. milk

Mix the first eight ingredients. In a separate bowl, beat together the rest of the ingredients. Combine the two mixtures. Bake in a 9x5-inch loaf pan, the inside bottom of which has been greased, for 50 minutes in a 350° F. oven.

Career Girl Sweet Potato Bread

$2\frac{3}{4}$ c. Mistress Biscuit Mix (see p. 5)
2 tsp. cinnamon
$\frac{3}{4}$ c. raisins
$\frac{1}{3}$ c. sugar
2 tbsp. olive *or* vegetable oil
1 c. cooked sweet potato, mashed
2 c. milk

Mix dry ingredients. In a separate bowl, mix wet ingredients. Combine the two mixtures and spoon into a 9x5-inch loaf pan, the inside bottom of which has been greased. Bake at 350° F. for approximately 45 minutes.

1927 PB Bread

This recipe is based on a 1927 magazine recipe. The children often request that I make this loaf. (I enjoy it, too!)

2 c. whole wheat flour
1 tbsp. baking powder
$^1/_2$ tsp. salt
$^1/_3$ c. sugar
$^1/_2$ c. peanut butter
$1^2/_3$ c. milk

Mix the dry ingredients. In a different bowl combine thoroughly the remaining ingredients. Stir together the two mixtures. Spoon into a loaf pan, the inside bottom of which has been greased; and bake at 350° F. for around 45 minutes, or until firm.

Peanut Butter Fun Bread

2 c. whole wheat flour
1 c. quick oats
1 tbsp. baking powder
$^1/_2$ tsp. salt
1 c. peanut butter
3 to 4 tbsp. brown sugar, packed
1 egg, beaten
$1^2/_3$ c. milk
$^1/_2$ to 1 c. raisins

Proceed as in the previous recipe; then bake for 60 to 70 minutes.

Healthy Hobo Bread

The next recipe is known by an intriguing name. (The original Hobo Bread called for white flour and lots of sugar, but I changed it.) I don't really think that hobos would happen to have all the ingredients for this bread, but I understand that they did bake bread in cans in the embers of their campfires.

1½ c. raisins
1⅓ c. boiling water
2 tsp. baking soda
3 tbsp. olive *or* vegetable oil
¼ c. sugar
½ tsp. salt
1 egg, beaten
2 c. whole wheat flour

Pour the boiling water over the raisins and add the baking soda; stir. Add oil, sugar, and salt. Let cool slightly. Add beaten egg and flour slowly. Spoon into three one-pound cans which have been well-greased. Bake in a 350° F. oven for 45 minutes or until firm.

Notes: Nuts and dates may be added. You may wish to remove the bottoms of the cans after the baked bread has completely cooled in order to get the bread out more easily. — My husband loves this bread . . . .

Applesauce Nut Bread

2½ c. whole wheat flour
2 tsp. baking powder
¼ tsp. salt
1 tsp. cinnamon
⅓ c. brown sugar, packed
¾ c. pecans *or* walnuts, chopped
1 c. applesauce
½ c. raisins
2 tbsp. olive *or* vegetable oil
1¼ c. milk

Stir together the first six ingredients. In a separate bowl, combine the remaining ingredients. Mix together the two mixtures, and spoon into a 9x5-inch loaf pan, the inside bottom of which has been greased. Bake at 350° F. for approximately 40 minutes or until firm.

Variations: Omit baking powder; use 1 tsp. baking soda. Use white sugar rather than brown. Add an additional $\frac{1}{2}$ tsp. cinnamon, $\frac{1}{2}$ tsp. allspice, and $\frac{1}{4}$ tsp. cloves.

Bran Banana Loaves

$1\frac{1}{4}$ c. banana, mashed (3 medium bananas)
2 c. buttermilk *or* sour milk
2 c. wheat bran
$\frac{2}{3}$ c. raisins
3 tbsp. olive *or* vegetable oil
$\frac{1}{3}$ c. brown sugar, packed
3 c. whole wheat flour
1 tbsp. baking powder
1 tsp. baking soda
$\frac{1}{2}$ tsp. salt
2 tsp. cinnamon

Combine the first six ingredients. Separately mix the remaining ingredients. Stir together the two mixtures, and spoon into two 8x4-inch bread pans, the inside bottoms of which have been greased. Bake at 350° F. for around 40 minutes, or until a toothpick inserted near the center comes out clean.

Banana Oat Bread

We eat enough bananas around this household for the place to be designated a monkey preserve!

* * *

$1\frac{1}{2}$ c. whole wheat flour
$1\frac{1}{2}$ c. oat bran

2 tsp. baking powder
$1/4$ tsp. salt
$1/2$ tsp. baking soda
$1/2$ tsp. nutmeg
$1/3$ c. sugar
1 c. milk or enough to moisten throughout and make "spoonable"
3 tbsp. olive *or* vegetable oil
2 c. ripe banana, mashed
1 c. nuts (pecans *or* walnuts), chopped

Mix dry ingredients. In a separate bowl beat together the remaining ingredients. Combine the two mixtures thoroughly, and spoon into a 9x5-inch loaf pan, the inside bottom of which has been greased. Bake at 350° F. for around 45 minutes.

Banana, Date, and Oat Bran Bread

3 c. oat bran
3 c. whole wheat flour
1 tbsp. baking powder
$1/2$ tsp. salt
2 tsp. cinnamon
$1/2$ c. sugar
1 c. chopped dates
1 tbsp. vanilla
$1^1/2$ c. banana, mashed
2 tbsp. olive *or* vegetable oil
$2^1/2$ c. milk (approx.)

Mix the dry ingredients. In a different bowl, mix the remaining ingredients. Combine the two groups, adding more milk if needed to make a moist batter. Spoon the batter into two 8x4-inch loaf pans, the inside bottoms of which have been greased. Bake at 350° F. for around 40 minutes, or until a toothpick inserted near the center of the loaves comes out unsticky.

Sister's Raisin Banana Bread

1 c. unbleached *or* all-purpose flour
1 ½ c. whole wheat flour
2 ½ tsp. baking powder
¼ tsp. cinnamon
¼ c. sugar
3 tbsp. olive *or* vegetable oil
1 tsp. vanilla
1 c. ripe banana, mashed
⅓ to 1 c. golden *or* dark raisins
¾ to 1 c. milk

Combine the dry things, then the wet things. Stir together. Spoon batter into a prepared 9x5-inch pan. Bake at 350° F. for approximately 40 minutes.

Apple-Hint Banana Bread

2 ½ c. flour (preferably whole wheat)
1 tsp. baking powder
1 tsp. baking soda
¼ tsp. salt
1 tsp. cinnamon
⅓ to ½ c. sugar
2 c. ripe banana, mashed
½ c. applesauce
1 tsp. vanilla
1 c. milk

Stir together the dry ingredients. In another bowl, thoroughly mix together the remaining four ingredients. Combine the two mixtures and spoon into a 9x5-inch loaf pan, the inside bottom of which has been greased. (If time permits, let the unbaked loaf sit 20 minutes or so before baking.) Bake at 350° F. for 50 minutes, or until a toothpick stuck into the center comes out clean.

Hints: After removing the loaf from the oven, sit it on a wire rack, cover with a clean kitchen towel, and let it cool a bit. When cool enough to handle, use a metal "pancake flipper" to gently remove the bread from the pan. Allow to cool completely, covered, sitting on the rack. Then put it into a plastic bag. — Best if allowed to "mellow" overnight before serving, at which time it can be re-heated.

Beer Bread with Currants

3 c. whole wheat flour (can use part unbleached *or* all-purpose flour)
1 tsp. baking powder
$^1/_2$ tsp. baking soda
2 tbsp. honey, molasses, *or* sugar
$^1/_2$ c. currants *or* raisins
1 (12-oz.) bottle of beer

Mix dry ingredients. Add beer. Stir only until dough is moistened and sticky. Pour into a 9x5-inch loaf pan, the inside bottom of which has been greased. Bake at 300° F. for 55 to 60 minutes.

I adore "cone bread" (a Southern drawl-ish way of saying "corn bread"). Here are some worthwhile entries:

Miller's Bran Corn Bread

Fiber-full and down-home good, this corn bread will fulfill your stomach's every yearning (at least for corn bread)!

* * *

$1^1/_2$ c. wheat bran
$1^1/_2$ c. cornmeal

1½ c. whole wheat flour
1 tbsp. baking powder
¾ tsp. salt
2 tbsp. olive *or* vegetable oil
¼ c. honey
2¼ to 2½ c. milk (enough to make a thick, but pourable batter)

Mix dry things. In a different bowl stir together liquids. Combine. Mix well and spoon into a greased 9x13x2-inch baking dish. Bake at 350° F. for about 30 minutes.

Kentucky Corn Bread

3 c. cornmeal
1 c. unbleached *or* all-purpose flour
1 tbsp. sugar
4 tsp. baking powder
1 tsp. salt
3 c. milk
¼ c. olive *or* vegetable oil

Proceed as in previous recipe.

Add-No-Fat Applesauce Corn Bread

1½ c. cornmeal
1½ c. unbleached *or* all-purpose flour
1 tbsp. baking powder
½ tsp. salt
¾ c. applesauce
1¼ c. milk

Combine the dry ingredients. In a separate bowl mix the applesauce and milk together. Stir together the two mixtures and spoon into a 9x5-inch loaf bread pan, the inside bottom of which has been greased. Bake at 350° F. for around 40 minutes.

Maize Mace Bread

2 c. whole wheat flour
1½ c. cornmeal
2 tsp. baking powder
½ tsp. salt
1 tsp. ground mace
2 tbsp. olive *or* vegetable oil
3 tbsp. honey
2¼ c. milk (or enough to create a wet, spoonable batter)
1 egg, beaten

Combine the dry ingredients. In a separate bowl combine the remaining ingredients. Stir together the two mixtures. Spoon batter into a prepared 9x5-inch loaf pan and bake at 350° F. for 40 minutes, more or less. (Test with a toothpick for doneness.)

Sleepy Hollow Corn Bread

The following recipe comes from Philipsburg Manor in New York's Hudson Valley, which is "Washington Irving country." Philipsburg Manor is a restored Dutch colonial site, once the location of an 18th-century trading center and country estate. The manor house there is built of stone, and there is an operating gristmill at which corn is water-ground between French burr millstones. This old-fashioned milling technique produces especially flavorful cornmeal. — Enjoy this corn bread, and dream of the gentleness of Sleepy Hollow.

* * *

1 c. unbleached *or* all-purpose flour
½ tsp. salt
4 tsp. baking powder
1 c. yellow cornmeal
¼ c. sugar
1 c. milk

2 eggs, beaten
1 tbsp. olive *or* vegetable oil

Combine the dry ingredients. In another container, mix the wet ingredients; then combine together the two mixtures. Spoon into a greased 8x8x2-inch pan and bake at 375° F. for 20 to 25 minutes, or until firm and lightly toasted around the edges.

Pain de Bran

The French call bran bread "pain de son" (pronounced "panh duh sonh"). "Pain de bran" (pronounced "panh duh branh") is my own fanciful appellation. A little French is a dangerous thing!

* * *

1 pkg. baking yeast
3½ c. warm water
4 c. wheat bran
2 tsp. salt
5 or more c. unbleached, bread, *or* all-purpose flour

Mix yeast, water, and bran. After ten minutes, add salt and flour. You will probably need to add *much* more flour. Knead well until soft and elastic. Let rise in a greased and covered bowl until double in volume. Shape into two loaves and let rise, covered, in greased bread pans until the dough rises to the tops of the pans. Bake in a preheated 375° F. oven for about 45 minutes.

Never Fail Wheat Bread

1 pkg. baking yeast
1¾ c. warm water
¼ c. brown sugar, packed
3 tbsp. olive *or* vegetable oil

1 tsp. salt
2 c. whole wheat flour
3 to 3 1/4 c. unbleached, bread, *or* all-purpose flour, sifted

Dissolve the yeast in the warm water with the brown sugar added. When it bubbles, add oil, salt, and whole wheat flour. Beat well. Gradually add enough white flour to make a workable dough. Form a ball; knead until silky smooth. Place in a greased bowl, rolling the ball around to grease all surfaces. Cover loosely. Let rise about an hour or until doubled. Punch down. Form two loaves. Place in well-greased bread pans. Let rise, covered lightly, in a warm spot. When the dough is taller than the sides of the pans, bake at 350° F. for about 40 minutes.

Relaxing Yeast Bread (No Knead)

2 c. whole wheat flour
2 c. unbleached *or* all-purpose flour
2 tbsp. sugar
1 tsp. salt
1 tbsp. baking yeast
2 c. warm water

Mix the first four ingredients. Dissolve yeast in 1 c. of water. Stir into dry ingredients. Add 1 c. water to make a soft dough. If necessary, add more warm water to moisten all the flour. Let the dough rise in a bowl until doubled. Divide and put into two greased 8x4-inch *glass* bread pans (not metal). Let rise until doubled. Bake at 400° F. for 40 minutes.

A Little Spice Yeast Bread

2 pkg. baking yeast
1/2 c. warm water
1/4 c. molasses, honey, *or* sugar
1 c. wheat bran
1 1/2 c. boiling water

$^1/_4$ c. olive *or* vegetable oil
$2^1/_2$ c. whole wheat flour
1 tsp. salt
$^1/_4$ tsp. cinnamon
$^1/_8$ tsp. ground mace
$1^1/_2$ to 2 c. unbleached *or* all-purpose flour

Dissolve the yeast in the warm water. Add sweetener. Meanwhile combine bran and boiling water; then add oil. When the mixture has cooled to lukewarm, add the yeast mixture; then, stir in wheat flour, salt, and spices. Gradually stir in enough white flour to form a soft, but kneadable dough. Knead well and place in a greased bowl. Cover the bowl and let rise in a warm place until doubled. Punch down and shape into two loaves. Place in greased bread pans. Cover and let rise until the dough comes up above the sides of the pans. Bake at 350° F. for approximately 40 minutes, or until the loaves sound hollow when tapped.

Oatmeal Yeast Bread

1 c. quick oats
2 c. boiling water
2 pkg. baking yeast
$^1/_3$ c. warm water
1 tsp. salt
$^1/_4$ c. honey
2 tbsp. olive *or* vegetable oil
3 c. whole wheat flour
2 to $2^1/_2$ c. unbleached *or* all-purpose flour

Soak oats in 2 cups boiling water. Let cool until lukewarm. Dissolve yeast in $^1/_3$ cup warm water. Add yeast, salt, honey and oil to oatmeal. Mix in flour, and knead until smooth. Place in greased bowl, cover and let rise until double in size. Place in two greased loaf pans or a bundt pan. Let rise about 2 hours or until well-risen. Bake at 350° F. for approximately 40 minutes.

A Final Word

Now scoot into your kitchen, stir up some bread, and bake someone happy! (A culminating thought: my children claim that you can plant bread crumbs to get more bread.)

Notes

[1] Jeffrey Steingarten, *The Man Who Ate Everything*, Alfred A. Knopf, New York, 1997, p. 330.

[2] *Ibid.*, p. 19.

[3] This recipe is provided by Teague's Mill, Gatlinburg, Tennessee.

[4] *Ibid.*

[5] Recipe courtesy Jodie Sullivan, Gretna, Virginia.

[6] Bill Neal, *Biscuits, Spoonbread, and Sweet Potato Pie*, Alfred A. Knopf, New York, 1990, p. 108.

[7] *The First Ladies Cook Book*, Parents' Magazine Press, New York, 1966, pp. 133-134.